wedding details

wedding details

mary norden

photography by polly wreford

RYLAND
PETERS
& SMALL
London New York

This book is dedicated to all brides to be.

Designer Catherine Griffin

Senior editor Annabel Morgan

Editor Sophie Bevan

Location research manager Kate Brunt

Production Patricia Harrington

Publishing director Alison Starling

Art director Gabriella Le Grazie

Stylist Mary Norden

First published in the United Kingdom in 2000.
This paperback edition first published in 2006 by
Ryland Peters & Small
20–21 Jockey's Fields
London WC1R 4BW
www.rylandpeters.com

10 9 8 7 6 5 4 3 2 1

Text © Mary Norden 2000, 2006
Design and photographs © Ryland Peters & Small 2000, 2006

ISBN-10: 1 84597 292 9
ISBN-13: 978 1 84597 292 9

A CIP record for this book is available from the British Library.

Printed and bound in China.

contents

introduction

*W*eddings have moved on since the days of calling in the professionals to do everything. Many brides take great pleasure in choosing and arranging flowers, wrapping up small tokens for guests to take home, and deciding on, or even making, the perfect gift to say thank you to the best man, bridesmaids and page boys.

In these pages you'll find ideas for everything from dressing the table for the wedding feast to choosing the flowers for the bouquet. You'll see how simple wrapping can transform humble but thoughtful wedding favours into desirable packages and discover novel ways to turn wedding ephemera like pressed flowers into exquisite keepsakes.

Every taste is catered for. From the cooly contemporary to the steadfastly traditional, you will find ideas that appeal and are sure to be inspired to add a few of your own.

classic wedding

The classic elegance of the white rose provided the inspiration for this stylish and traditional celebration. The creamy-white colour theme was carried throughout, enlivened with touches of glossy green foliage for contrast and flashes of gilt to enhance the sophisticated effect.

Above and top: Each place setting includes an intriguing gift box, plus a white rose to echo the centrepieces and overall wedding theme.

Right: At the wedding table, all-white china can be a little severe. Include touches of pattern here and there, like the decorative foliage borders on these soup dishes. Starched white damask napkins folded into a triangle and rolled up, present a neat fold for a name card to be slipped inside.

Don't make your guests lean around flowers
to chat across the table. Instead, choose
low-level conversation-friendly centrepieces.

Crisp starched napkins are both beautiful and practical.
Fold them to hold breadsticks for each place setting, to
serve with soup. By using plain white napkins you
repeat the chosen colour theme, and a sprig of foliage
tucked into the folds adds contrast.

For the centrepiece, use a wreath of florist's oasis,
hidden with foliage and scattered with a few white
roses. Don't be overly lavish with the roses – erring on

The frothy foliage and sophisticated lime-green flowers of bupleurum provide contrast and link different areas of the table setting. Tiny sprigs are arranged randomly against the pristine icing of the wedding cake (above) and tucked into napkins (far left), while longer stems are a perfect foil for the flawless white roses of the centrepiece (left).

Both contrasting and toning elements keep a classic theme going successfully, from the wide white satin bows used to decorate the dining chairs (right), to the pattern of heavy silver cutlery (below) and the delicate designs on the china (bottom).

the side of caution is more in keeping with a classic yet simple wedding reception.

To add an element of surprise to the decorative theme of the wedding tables, why not serve one course on patterned china? Don't worry if you don't have enough plates or bowls in one design to serve all your guests; use a different pattern for each table.

You can also add touches of colour and texture in a variety of unexpected ways – heavy antique silver cutlery with an embossed pattern, for example, or the contrasting ribbon used to fasten the ribbed-card gift boxes.

The boxes here have been tied with two types of ribbon, layered one on top of the other. A plain green satin ribbon is topped with a length of dainty braiding in lime green, picking up the colour contrast between the leaves and flowers of the bupleurum sprigs scattered about the tables.

The details on the bridal gown — even the toe or heel of a slipper — can reflect the spirit of the whole day.

Above and right: Every bride should have the outfit of her dreams. From a border encrusted with beads to the elegantly embroidered columns of the bride's slippers, not a single detail should be overlooked. Delicate beading, buttoning and embroidery are all ways of adding style without being ostentatious. Using self-coloured thread, beads and buttons adds opulence while being discreet.

Left and above: Dress the bridesmaids to provide a beautiful backdrop for the bride. These shades of coffee-coloured taffeta will complement the bridal gown perfectly. A big faux flower slipped into the sash looks suitably extravagant and is much more robust than the real thing. Save proper roses for the bridesmaids' posies.

17

table settings

The table is the place where guests will probably spend much of their time, especially at a formal wedding breakfast or dinner. Although setting the table is likely to be the last of your tasks, it creates a vital first impression as people arrive. Making an effort to create original ideas for name cards, napkins and flowers is time well spent. Buffet tables, too, offer plenty of scope for decoration.

napkins

Napkins are vital to protect delicate dresses and smart suits from splashes and spills, but they also give you an opportunity to use your imagination when deciding how to present them. Choosing the very best quality napkins will add simple elegance to place settings, and – whether you go for fine linen tightly rolled, starched damask folded to form a fan or gauzy organza dropped over a wine glass like a fallen parachute – to be really useful, the napkin should be generous in size. Accessories and dressings should be simple but striking, such as garden greenery and lengths of ribbon.

Above: The original folds of this sheer organza add substance to the shape. Sugared almonds complete the look.
Right: Starched damask is coaxed into pleats then nipped in at the centre with ribbon and a simple spray.

Left: To make these napkin rings, cut wide satin ribbon into 20cm lengths. Write names on paper that is not too stiff; cut into rectangles and attach to the ribbon with spray glue. Wrap each length around a napkin and secure with glue or double-sided tape. Adding a sprig of rosemary not only looks decorative, it smells divine.

Above: A single flower laid on a folded napkin adds instant elegance with precious little preparation.

21

Welcome friends and family to the wedding
feast: a well-laid table not only looks
inviting but makes your guests feel special.

This page: A starched damask napkin has been cleverly folded so that a name card can be neatly slipped under the top fold, while a single scabious (Scabiosa) flower makes a simple adornment.

Opposite: Cutlery rolled in a napkin ready for a buffet and tied with a simple twist of ribbon, is casual yet stylish.

23

name cards

Novel ideas for name cards aren't hard to come up with. If you have a little time to spare, you can make some witty and unusual pointers to direct guests to their seats. For a lavish wedding, you might use a labelled favour. At a more relaxed event, chocolate name flags are good fun. You can either print off names on a computer or write them neatly yourself. A classic italic script suits a formal wedding: it's easy to read with just a hint of a flourish. More ornate scripts can be difficult to decipher.

Left: To make these chocolate name flags, cut short lengths of wire-edged ribbon. Cut a fishtail at one end and attach double-sided tape to the other. Place a cocktail stick on the tape and roll inwards to secure. Then cut the paper with the names on into rectangles, glue each one onto the ribbon and push the cocktail stick into a chocolate for a base.

Marie

This page and centre: Name cards can be as lavish or as effortless as you want them to be. Set a wrapped favour at each place setting and use the label as a name card, or simply lay a handwritten card in a beautiful cup and saucer.

Camilla

Xavier

Far left: Cupcake cases filled with glossy redcurrant berries add a touch of vivid colour to an all-white table setting. A handwritten name card has been casually slipped in.

Centre: Half a lemon is wrapped in pristine white muslin tied with white cotton tape to which a name card is attached. This is ideal if you are serving a starter that requires lemon.

Right: A tiny bunch of trimmed asparagus is tied with satin ribbon threaded through a name card and perched on top of each wineglass.

centrepieces

A table needs a focal point, and flowers have always been the conventional choice. For something just a bit different, arrangements of candles or extravagantly presented food can look striking, too. Take into account the formality of the occasion and the style of the menu being served, and choose a centrepiece accordingly. For a round table, a single centrepiece is ideal. On a long narrow table, you may want to repeat a series of arrangements throughout its length.

Glass cakestands come in many designs, from the ornately frilly to the severely classical, and can be used in the centre of the table to hold all sorts of sweets, biscuits and fruits, not just cakes. Candles, too, make beautiful centrepieces. Thick pillar candles running the entire length of the table or an arrangement of floating

Above: Narcissus flowers are tucked between frosted lemons in a glass compote.
Centre left: An enticing array of petit fours on a two-tier stand, made by simply standing a smaller dish on top of a larger one.

Centre right: A bell-shaped Italian cake presented on a silver tray and tied with white ribbon makes an unusual centrepiece.
Opposite: White and silver sugared almonds fill a Victorian fluted glass dish.

candles will bring a fairy-tale charm to the setting. Alternatively, you could choose the soothing flicker of decorated nightlights or a radiant display of tapers. But bear in mind that fancy designs and strident colours are out of place at an elegantly set table. For maximum impact, restrict your choice to white or ivory candles and plain column shapes to enhance the overall effect.

Far left: This strikingly patterned bowl filled with white roses makes a sumptuous centrepiece. The pink-and-white theme can be repeated throughout the table with pink napkins and favour boxes tied with matching pink ribbon.

Left: Glass desert bowls each hold a single orchid and combine with candles to form an exotic display.

Above: A delicate china cakestand holds a thick pillar candle, surrounded by a carpet of rose petals and scattered narcissus flowers.

31

Conjure an air of romance and intimacy with a display of twinkling candlelight.

Above and left: Surround and emphasize a central vase with elegantly trimmed nightlights. Simply attach narrow pleated ribbon to their metal dishes using double-sided tape.

Opposite: Tiny candles set afloat on a sea of scented rose petals make a luminous centrepiece at twilight.

Above: A handful of tapers stand in a white china bowl, filled with a wedge of soaked florist's oasis to hold the candles in place and frothing with greeny-white cow parsley and sophisticated white Nerine. Tapers burn quickly, so aim to light them later in the meal, perhaps to celebrate the speeches or toasts.

chair backs

Chair backs offer extra potential for decorating a room and have been relatively under used until recently. There is something very charming and quite unexpected about a chair embellished with a tied posy or trimmed with a great gauzy ribbon. Pay special attention to the bride's and groom's chairs, and use simpler ideas for the rest of the seating, if you prefer. Choose long-lasting flowers that will look good all day.

Hydrangeas are a good option as their papery flowers last well.

Left: A simple paper cone overflows with green and white variegated foliage and a froth of humble cow parsley, tied with wide satin ribbon.
Above: A single diaphanous bow of palest yellow organdie softens this painted chair back.
Right: The washed-out sky blue of a mophead hydrangea is partnered with a narrow pale blue ribbon on a white bentwood chair.

Remember to fasten ribbons tightly so
that they don't slip rakishly to one side
or, worse, spill their posies.

Fine accessories for the wedding table: a bone china coffee cup with a subtle handpainted gold scroll design (top); silver forks with pearly handles and embossed shanks (above); dinner plates with striking coloured borders (right), and a row of elegant silver-topped salt cellars (far right).

table accessories

People eat with their eyes first, so presentation at the table is as important as the food that is served. Plain plates with a coloured border frame food elegantly, while the shiniest, sparkliest glasses do justice to the wines offered. As with all very special occasions, it pays to be extravagant to achieve the effect you want. A well-orchestrated table reflects the special day and quality really stands out – fine table linens, real silverware, crystal glasses and bone china coffee cups are unmistakable.

cakes

The cake can set the tone of the whole wedding. A classic three-tiered cake finished in smooth white icing is a blank canvas waiting to be decorated, so let your inspiration flow. Instead of getting all tangled up with complicated loops and swirls of conventional piped icing, a fresher and more contemporary look can be achieved by using ribbons and real flowers. For a winter wedding, when appropriate flowers can be scarce, a simple scattering of velvet blossoms is pretty and informal, while skeins of ivy would look darkly dramatic. In autumn, dahlias and wild berries would make bold and bright decorations.

A three-tiered iced cake is treated in three different ways, yet retains an overall simplicity of style.
Left: A generous trail of gauzy ribbon and a random sprinkling of pale pastel velvet flowers provide an effortlessly pretty look.

Above: A glamorous single rose is the ultimate in understated elegance.
Right: Broad bands of ribbon, an exotic orchid and a few scattered silver and white sugared almonds combine for a smart, sophisticated cake.

contemporary
wedding

A contemporary wedding utilizes modern elements but doesn't dispense with tradition altogether. Here classic white is combined with bold greens to achieve the desired look. Striking sculptural flowers, unusual grasses, streamlined glassware and simple white china all contribute to the overall effect.

The colour scheme for this contemporary wedding still makes use of classic white, but the main impression is created by strongly contrasting green – and the way in which the colours have been combined makes it unmistakably modern. Green is an ideal theme for contemporary weddings, especially during the winter months, when fresh flowers are scarce and prices rise accordingly. Exotic flowers and grasses are widely available even in the depths of winter, as they are flown in from countries with a tropical climate. Here, they create a very different and original look, reinforced by the modern table setting where everything is streamlined and simple.

Above: Bold napkin rings can be made from flat glossy leaves rolled around napkins and tied in place with a few flexible grass stems.

Opposite: There is no distracting tablecloth and all the glassware and china has clean graphic lines, from the cylindrical salt and pepper pots to the alternating frosted-glass vases and candleholders.

Left: The tropical painter's palette flower (Anthurium) has a bold sculptural shape complemented by the exuberant fountains of bear grass (Dasylirion). Although both are green in colour, they couldn't be more different in form and texture.

Left and opposite: Pliable grasses can be used instead of ribbon to tie favours or to hold a rolled-up menu. Use several strands of different shades of green for contrast. Here the menus have been printed on thick tracing paper, but greaseproof paper would work well too.

Left: Small succulent plants like sedum or echeveria can be potted in decorative containers for alternative table arrangements. Spray small terracotta pots with silver paint (two thin coats are better than one thick one). When dry, plant up and finish with a silver ribbon. These would also make pretty and long-lasting mementoes for guests to take home.

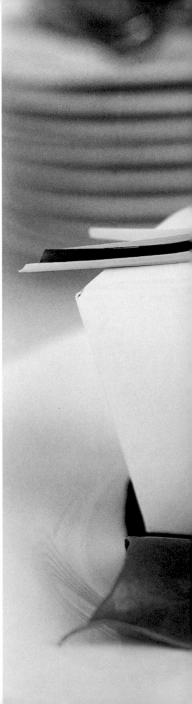

Keep flower arrangements simple. Just a few well-chosen blooms carefully presented can outshine a meadow's worth of flowers.

Far left: The pure clean lines of arum lilies (Zantedeschia aethiopica) are breathtaking in their simplicity. Flowers such as these and painter's palettes, both of which have strong outlines, create maximum impact arranged alone or with an absolute minimum of added foliage. Their strong graphic shapes make them especially suitable for modern, minimalist interiors.

Left: Waiters in simple, informal dress suit a wedding reception in a contemporary setting.

47

flowers

As soon as the date is set, check which flowers will be in season. There are good reasons for sticking to seasonal blooms: not only will costs be lower but the flowers will also be more robust if they are at their peak. Let the bride's and bridesmaids' dresses guide you when choosing flower colours. Today, anything goes – from traditional white or cream to pink, apricot or even bold reds and purples.

bouquets

After the bride's gown, the flowers the bride carries are the next most important consideration. The bouquet's composition, colour and shape will set the tone for all the other flowers needed for the day.

Thankfully, rules of etiquette for wedding flowers have long been ignored. What matters is what you want – flowers should reflect your taste, plus the season and the style of the location. The bouquet can be an elaborate florist's arrangement or a simple posy gathered from your own garden on the morning of the wedding. It may use flowers in tones that reflect the colour of the gown or be a wild cascade of fiery colours for extra drama.

Left: A single orchid stem makes a dramatic statement.
Right: A handful of old-fashioned garden roses create a sweetly scented and romantic bouquet.

Left: Three flawless arum lilies, loosely tied, make a minimalist bouquet, perfect for a simple silk gown and a contemporary setting. For maximum drama, just one single lily could be carried.

Right and above: The polar opposite of pure white flowers – an unusual bouquet in shades of tawny orange and red. The orchids here are spotted with red that echoes the sprays of tiny red berries, and the stems are tied with a more traditional cream satin ribbon.

The simplest fragrant
handful tied with a
ribbon brings an extra
touch of romance to the
bride's outfit.

Opposite: When choosing flowers for a bouquet, aim to capture the season as well as the style and atmosphere of the wedding. Here a simple bunch of white longi lillies (Lilium longiflorum) mixed with tails of white loosestrife (Lysimachia clethroides) has an air of summer elegance.

This page: The softest, dreamiest and palest flowers are often a bride's first choice. This loosely tied posy of full-blown, creamy white ranunculus is subtle in colour and romantic in style.

buttonholes

Buttonholes have come a long way since the obligatory carnation on a pin. With a little imagination, it's possible to fashion a buttonhole from almost any plant. Flowers aren't vital – a spray of greenery can look equally smart, and most gardens will yield a surprising selection, from rosemary to ivy to lilac. For a formal wedding, a rose beautifully dressed with a satin ribbon is the romantic's choice, while for a relaxed country occasion, a sprig of lime-green lady's mantle (Alchemilla mollis) looks charming. Whatever you choose, remove any thorns or prickles and wrap stems in florist's tape before binding with ribbon and adding a simple bow.

From left: Sprigs of white lilac (Syringa) with ribbon and braid; bold, variegated ivy with contrasting purple ribbon; rosemary sprigs – with or without flowers – are an aromatic choice; kangaroo paw (Anigozanthos) has long-lasting flower trumpets.
Right: A spray of white-flowered viburnum – a popular garden shrub – wrapped in ribbon for a delicate buttonhole.

57

table flowers

The most effective table arrangements are created by limiting the types of flowers to two or three species – or even just one. Simple themes are the easiest to put together and also the most inexpensive. Containers are important, too, and should be chosen to suit the flowers. Elegant lilies need a streamlined vase, while informal cottage-garden posies could be presented in containers concealed by rustic baskets. Remember to keep all arrangements low for uninterrupted cross-table talk.

Far left: A series of individual arrangements can be used to decorate the table; here a single orchid flower floats in a Victorian glass dessert dish.

Centre: Flat scabious heads packed tightly into a glass vase make a satisfyingly rounded dome of flowers.

Left: A soup tureen is just the right height for a central arrangement of soft, papery hydrangea heads spiked with pink blooms of double lisianthus (Eustoma grandiflorum).

Fill shiny pails with a mass of frothy variegated foliage and a lacy topping of dill flowers.

Opposite and below: Miniature galvanized buckets are ideal for individual arrangements. Line them with one or two layers of white tissue paper, then add a layer of plastic cut from a carrier bag and use soaked

florist's foam to hold the flowers and foliage. Trim any plastic showing before setting them on the table.
Left: A small terracotta pot painted silver and filled with toning grey-green foliage and silvery-blue thistles, held in place using florist's foam.

The finished effect, using a large central arrangement echoed by individual ones at each place setting. These tiny galvanized buckets are hard to beat as flower containers: they're inexpensive, stylish and their shiny finish suits a cream and green colour scheme. The combination of variegated foliage and greeny-white flowers is imaginative and sophisticated.

floral wedding

Flowers are a focal point at an intimate wedding for family and close friends. Working on a small scale gives you the opportunity to be lavish with flowers. The blooms used here — paper-white narcissi and indigo hyacinths — are quite modest garden flowers, but massing them together looks extravagant.

The blue dining room at the wedding venue made easy work of deciding a colour scheme. A timeless mix of blue and cream is emphasized with pale blue linen napkins, creamy white china and tablecloths, and a combination of similarly coloured flowers. The overall effect is charming and effortless – the ideal atmosphere for a low-key, relaxed wedding. If you have time to plan ahead, instead of using cut flowers, plant up pots with bulbs and coax them into bloom in time by bringing them in from the cold a few weeks before the wedding.

Left: The table is set with terracotta flower pots painted white and brimming over with a heady mix of narcissi and hyacinths. The flowers are arranged in glass jam jars, hidden from view inside the pots.

Far left: Unfussy folded napkins and plain china and glassware set the tone for a small gathering of family and friends.
Above: A humble garden bench spruced up with a coat of paint makes an informal dining-room seat.

Continue the colour theme throughout the house or venue with the use of generous bows and carefully placed arrangements.

Left and right: Large bunches of narcissi or daffodils look wonderful on their own. Put them into a big container and you have a simple arrangement in an instant. Old-fashioned enamel pails are ideal, in classic white with navy blue trim or a more unusual shade of pale blue. Stand them casually at the foot of the stairs or by the door. **Top:** An alternative way to present the napkins, tied with gingham bows.

favours

Favours need not be elaborate or expensive. The best are often simple

gifts, imaginatively wrapped and presented. Send your guests home

with memories of a very special day and a tiny memento to say

thank you for coming — you'll be following a tradition that

can be traced back to ancient Rome.

edible

Favours based on sweets and foods are always popular. Dragees – almonds in a sugar coating – are traditional wedding favours: the nuts symbolize fertility as they are the seeds of the almond tree, and the combination of bitter almonds and sweet coating represents the 'for better and for worse' part of the wedding vows. Home-made biscuits, chocolates, parcels of nuts and even fruit can all be given as mementoes. The perfect time to serve edible favours is with after-dinner coffee – though you then run the risk that they may not last long enough to be taken home.

Right: Small chocolate-filled bags are folded from matte gold paper, tied with cream organza and satin ribbon and finished with a beaded berry. **Opposite:** Cellophane cones are filled with white jelly beans and tied with a flourish of mint-green ribbon.

Fitting mementoes of a special day — edible
wedding favours need to be not only delicious,
but beautifully dressed, too.

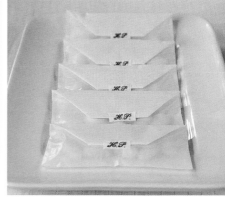

Above and left: Glassine bags – the semi-opaque paper envelopes used to protect photographic negatives and transparencies – make ideal wrappings for favours. Here they have been lined with an additional layer of lacy Japanese paper and filled with sugared almonds. The finishing touch is the snippet of name tape embroidered with the couple's initials and used to seal the bag.

Far left: White bonbons make a pretty alternative to sugared almonds. To wrap, cut circles of cellophane, place a handful in the centre, bring up the edges and tie with ribbon. You could also wrap them in circles of dressmaker's net or tulle, but leave the cellophane layer in place to stop powdered sugar leaking.

The easiest way to give every guest
a piece of wedding cake is to box
slices for them to take home. Cartons
are sold ready-made for the purpose –
just pile the filled boxes on an antique
serving platter placed near the door
so guests can help themselves as they
leave. Here, clusters of snowberries
(Symphoricarpos) have been tucked
between the boxes for decoration.

non-edible

A favour can be as simple as a bundle of candles or handful of spring bulbs to plant at home: it's the novelty of the gift that makes it memorable. Packaging doesn't have to be elaborate; it can be simple but still look stylish. Glassine bags are ideal for loose items, while boxes make awkwardly shaped gifts neater and easier to handle. At an Easter wedding, a hollowed egg handpainted with the initials of the bride and groom would make a simple but unusual parting gift.

Far left: Bundles of fine hand-dipped candles secured with satin cord and presented to guests on a silver platter make novel favours to take home.

Centre left: Boxes of delicate corrugated card can be used to hold spring or summer bulbs for a long-lasting memento.

Left: Glassine bags used to wrap bars of extra-special scented soap. Use a hole punch to perforate the top of the bag, fold it over and thread ribbon through the hole to secure.

Plain white paper bags filled with loose tea make charming wedding favours to take home. Choose an out-of-the-ordinary blend or something exotic. Fold down the bags to resemble a rectangular envelope and fasten with narrow ribbon. Arrange the favours in neat rows along bands of wide satin ribbon (inset) or pile them casually under a vase of flowers on a hall table or sideboard (main picture).

Wedding favours express your gratitude and serve to remind friends and family of their participation in the wedding.

Left: Sometimes the packaging is as important as the contents. These favour boxes may hold cookies, soaps or miniature scented candles. Whatever the contents, they are intriguingly embellished.

Above: Flower seeds repackaged in smart luxurious envelopes will bring results to be enjoyed long after the wedding is over.

Right: Special messages or photographs rolled in scrolls of tracing paper make very personal souvenirs of a wonderful day. Pile them in a glass dish and let guests help themselves.

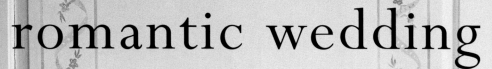

romantic wedding

This location provided the inspiration for a truly romantic wedding. The walls are embellished with a discreet, delicate ribbon and flower motif and even the chairs are shapely and curvaceous. Thick damask cloths, fine bone china, filigreed glasses and sugar-pink flowers carry the theme right through to the dining table.

Pink is a romantic, very feminine colour and a favourite choice for wedding bouquets and table settings. For pure romance, old-fashioned softer colours work best: think of the delicate shades of pale pink sweet peas and peonies. Some roses and tulips come in much hotter pinks for vibrant arrangements that will make a bolder statement. Use pink at the table for the flowers and repeat hints of the colour in the wrapping for favours or ribbon-tied napkins. A table laid for an intimate wedding feast, as shown here, could easily be scaled up to accommodate more guests at a larger wedding. Lots of small circular tables can be used to seat people instead of

Above: The romantic details at the table include a glass compote full of ribbon-wrapped favours, an elegant carafe and extravagant pink flowers.
Left: Pink hydrangeas and double lisianthus are an unconventional but pretty choice for wedding flowers. Cutting the stems low creates a full, rounded arrangement that focuses attention on the flowers.

one large table, and smaller chairs are an option if space around the tables becomes limited.

Little, unexpected touches can reinforce a theme with surprising emphasis. The curves and mouldings of a pretty painted chair, a tablecloth that elegantly sweeps the floor – elements that say romance out loud. Make use of these and similar details throughout the dining room and wedding location to set the tone for the day.

Left: Chiffon bows tied to door handles, a tiny posy casually laid on a pushed back chair – if the details are perfect, everything will fall into place.

Above and right: Oyster-coloured ribbon and a flushed bloom complete each table setting.

Far right: The delicate pastels of the wall decoration inspired the choice of colours for the wedding flowers.

Not so long ago, the cake — like the bride — could only be dressed in white. But what could be more appropriate for a romantic wedding than a blush of pink icing and a shower of bright blossoms?

The three-tiered cake is set on its own
table in the window, on a damask
cloth to match that of the main table.
Individual hydrangea florets have
been used to decorate the cake –
these could be saved and pressed
between the pages of a book, then
used to adorn thank-you cards and
letters, to remind guests of the
wedding flowers.

Many brides dream of a truly romantic wedding with a very feminine emphasis. Seize every opportunity to add as much romance to the special day as you can.

From left: Satin slingbacks with extravagant feather bows make fairy-tale bridal slippers; antique champagne flutes, etched with romantic vines and flowers, are served on a precious silver tray; a candle sconce garlanded with crystal drops casts the most flattering light of all.

93

finishing touches

Use these tiny but all-important details to personalize a wedding and add your own indelible style to the day. Here you'll find ideas for confetti, gifts for your bridesmaids and other important attendants, plus ring bags and cushions. Some will involve a little sewing or advance preparation; others are simply a question of presentation.

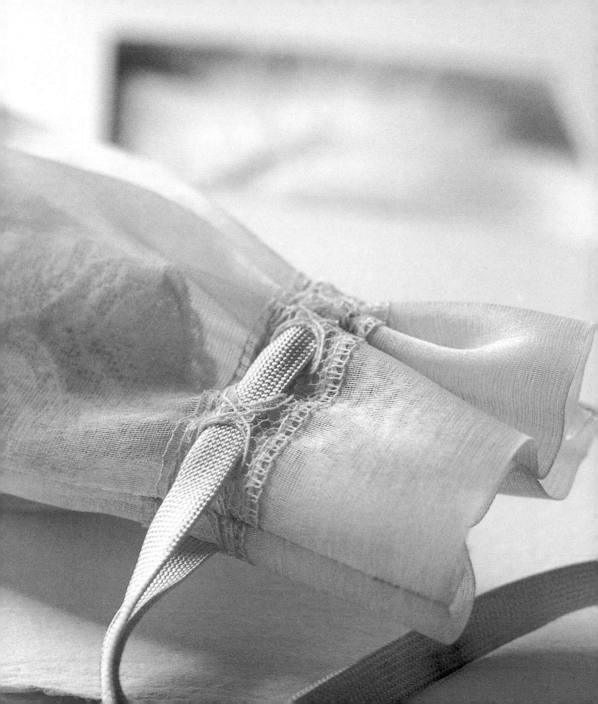

confetti

Ready-made confetti can be poor quality and mass-produced in predictable pastel colours. It's far more fun to make your own. Flower petals, rose petals in particular, are the obvious and perhaps the most romantic choice. If you are picking flowers from your own garden, cut them early in the morning when they are at their freshest, so the petals will still look their best later in the day. If you need a large quantity of confetti, one trick is to eke out rose petals by mixing them with large tissue-paper shapes.

Birdseed is another popular choice, but looks better presented in pretty packages. Pile bags, cones or boxes of confetti onto a large tray or into a basket and leave it by the door of the wedding venue, so that guests can pick up a package after the service.

Opposite: For an informal country wedding, an old enamelled pail has been filled with freshly picked rose petals and tiny flower heads. The bucket can be passed around so that every guest can take a handful.

Above left and right: Cones of handmade paper make charming containers for confetti. Alternatively, fill small cardboard sweet boxes with petals and secure with a ribbon until the contents are needed.

Always check beforehand with the venue or the church that confetti is permitted — some object to the debris left behind.

Parchment envelopes, the simple wooden punnets that strawberries are sold in, even miniature galvanized buckets – all these can be used to hold home-made or repackaged confetti. Flower petals are the ultimate biodegradable confetti, though they won't disappear overnight – unlike birdseed, which is guaranteed to. Avoid using rice confetti out of doors as it can be harmful to birds if swallowed.

Far left: Glassine bags perforated with a hole punch and secured with a twist of raffia keep birdseed confetti from spilling. These bags have been stacked on a Chinese bamboo sieve – a shiny silver tray or a shallow basket would work well too.

Left: A wicker basket normally used for carrying wine bottles is ideal for holding paper cones of confetti.

Top: A pleated pin-tucked silk satin ring bag tied with velvet ribbon.

Above: A ring cushion of textured wool, trimmed with silk picot edging and a central button.

Right and far right: An unusual stitched button or a Chinese bead make ideal fastenings for a ring bag.

ring bags and cushions

Don't let the best man go through the ritual of patting each pocket in turn
to find the rings. If you make a ring bag, he'll be able to tell immediately
where it is. All you need is a remnant or two of exquisite fabric – perhaps
left over from the bride's dress – plus an unusual bead or button and a
scrap of silk cord or ribbon. If you prefer, stitch a ring cushion for the page
boy to carry instead. Either way, you won't need a sewing machine – all
these ideas are simple to sew by hand.

gifts for attendants

The giving of presents to say thank you to attendants is an ancient tradition. In the whirlwind build-up to your wedding day, it is easy to lose sight of what the day means to all those around you, so remember your bridesmaids, flower girl, best man and page boy with gifts to show how much you appreciate their participation. Gifts can range from the simplest embroidered hankies or lavender sachets to grander offerings such as jewellery, or something very personal such as a first edition of a favourite book. Whatever you give, it should be an enduring memento of a lovely day: this is one instance where edible gifts aren't really appropriate.

Above: A gift of tiny monogrammed pillows filled with fragrant lavender.
Right: Take as much care in wrapping the gift as you did in buying it. Layers of ribbon and a velvet flower turn a package from functional to beautiful.

Above: If giving small pieces of jewellery such as cuff links or earrings, keep an eye open for unusual boxes like this 1930s pill box. Line it with tissue paper to hold the jewellery, but there's no need to wrap the box: it looks quite intriguing as it stands.
Left: Lavender sachets made from exquisitely embroidered linen can be an awkward shape to wrap, so are more easily packaged in a cardboard sweet box.

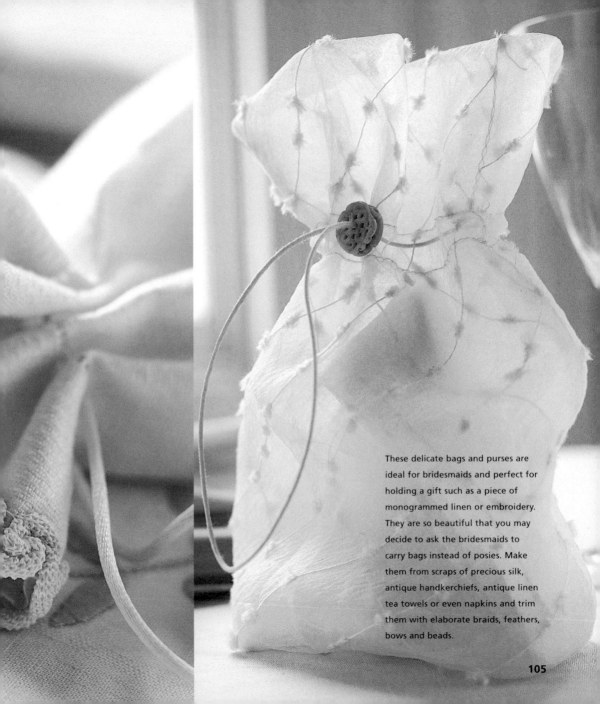

These delicate bags and purses are ideal for bridesmaids and perfect for holding a gift such as a piece of monogrammed linen or embroidery. They are so beautiful that you may decide to ask the bridesmaids to carry bags instead of posies. Make them from scraps of precious silk, antique handkerchiefs, antique linen tea towels or even napkins and trim them with elaborate braids, feathers, bows and beads.

*Say thank you in the most personal
way. Indulge your bridesmaids and
other attendants with gifts that can
be used again and again.*

Translucent mother-of-pearl egg spoons make exquisite gifts to say thank you to wedding attendants. You could add an initialled egg cup to make the present complete. A pair of antique silver-lidded mother-of-pearl pepper and salt pots would make an elegant alternative.

country wedding

An informal country wedding followed by a buffet set out in the village hall is one

of the most relaxed ways to celebrate a marriage. Despite the effortless appearance

of the table and the food, careful planning is still essential to make the day

a success. As always, the little details — the sweep of the checked

cloth over the linen, the bunches of lavender — are all important.

Wire baskets of bread, bottles of olive oil and luscious figs set a table as generous and bountiful as a harvest supper. Sprigs of fresh lavender tied with lilac ribbon to decorate napkins and informal arrangements of white loosestrife (Lysimachia clethroides) and ranunculus standing in old-fashioned plain jugs add to the relaxed atmosphere.

111

This page: The elements of a rustic wedding: good bread laid straight onto the cloth as they would in France, rich fruity olive oil for dipping and simple cottage-garden flowers. **Opposite:** Dress all tables to match the buffet, with similar cloths and flowers.

If you cannot find colourful tablecloths to buy or hire, it's easy to make your own – and that way you'll get exactly what you want. A simple hem transforms a length of fabric into the tablecloth of your choice. Lay the patterned cloth over plain white linen and scoop it up in the centre; secure the gathers with a safety pin and add a bundle of lavender and a lilac satin bow to form a focal point.

When guests help themselves from a buffet the majority will stand and eat. However, it's a good idea to have a few small tables dotted around the room as some people may prefer to sit down.

Have candles to hand as dusk falls.
Sheltering in storm lanterns or glass jars,
their soothing flickers cast a warm glow.

114

Far left: Modest wooden punnets hold a fragrant mix of rice and lavender confetti. Remember that rice should not be thrown where birds might eat it.
Centre: Dress plain chairs to match the table, using two bunches of lavender tied end to end. Disguise the join with a lilac satin sash.
Above: These galvanized mesh storm lanterns light the way on the stairs. Place others at strategic points, on windowsills and tables, and outdoors, at gate posts and along paths.

115

keepsakes

Photographs are the most literal reminders of a happy day, but all sorts of objects can become treasured mementoes. There are bound to be keepsakes from the day that you want to store safely alongside the photographs. Here are some ideas for keepsakes for the bride and groom and to send to close friends and family.

Below: Send wedding pictures framed in a home-made card, folded in three so the front two flaps open like window shutters. Line them with tissue and add ribbons to fasten.

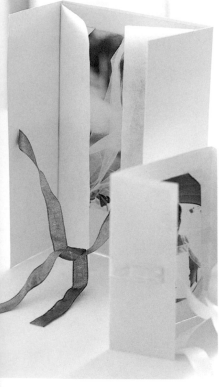

Careful storage of mementoes will ensure that your wedding memories last a lifetime. Photographs should be kept in complete darkness to prevent fading, and one way to store them safely is to make a wedding portfolio. This is a much more informal way of keeping and displaying photographs than a traditional heavy leather album. Add other treasured memories such as menus, sheet music, telegrams from absent friends and family, the notes from the best man's speech and the order of the service – anything that is important to you.

Above: To make a portfolio, bind two large pieces of card together along the spine with cream-coloured tape and tape across the corners too – for extra protection as well as decoration. Make a slit on each outer edge of card and thread ribbon through, securing one end on the inside with a dab of glue or piece of tape.

Make thank-you cards using pressed leaves from the bouquet. Tear out three rectangles of thick artist's watercolour paper and fold in half. Stitch them together through the centre then tie with velvet cord and use spray glue to attach leaves to the pages.

Individual keepsake albums to send to friends and family can be made from thick artist's watercolour paper tied with narrow ribbon. Cut a window in the cover to reveal a photo, a tiny pleated paper fan, a scrap of sheet music or buttons from the bride's or bridesmaid's dresses.

Pressed flowers and leaves taken from the bride's bouquet, scraps of fabric, exquisite trimmings, even buttons, can all spark happy memories.

After the whirl of the day, you will be left with wonderful memories. Cherish every one of these with precious mementoes. A very personal and visual collection of keepsakes can be displayed on an artist's canvas stretched over a frame, as shown here. You could include buttons, cufflinks, squares of fabric, skeins of embroidery thread, special trimmings – such as lace, cord and braid – earrings, buckles, and even tiny pockets of birdseed confetti. Include anything that holds special memories – it's entirely up to you.

Old-fashioned luggage tags have been used to frame and attach all sorts of trinkets, each hung from the string of the tag and further secured with a pin.

123

stockists

This is by no means a fully comprehensive list of suppliers, but my own personal list of favourite haunts where I go to be inspired and to find things to use, many of which are featured throughout the book.

Cakes

The British Sugarcraft Guild
Wellington House
Messeter Place
Eltham
London SE9 5DP
020 8859 6943
www.bsguk.org
They will put you in touch with cakemakers in your area.

Dunn's of Crouch End
6 The Broadway
Crouch End
London N8 9SN
020 8340 1614
www.dunns-bakery.co.uk
This long-established cakemaker made all the wedding cakes shown in this book. They deliver in London and the Home Counties.

Candles

Candle Makers' Supplies
28 Blythe Road
London W14 OHA
020 7602 4031/2
www.candlemakers.co.uk
Catalogue and mail order available.

Price's Candles
100 York Road
London SW11 3RU
020 7924 6336
www.prices-candles.co.uk

Confetti

Mary Jane Vaughan at Fast Flowers
Call 020 7385 8400 for mail order. Freeze-dried rose petals.

Masquerade
Call 0121 778 3455 for mail order. Rose-petal confetti.

Ribbons, trimmings and fabrics

The Bead Shop
21a Tower Street
London WC2H 9NS
020 7240 0931
www.beadshop.co.uk

Berwick Street Cloth Shop
14 Berwick Street
London W1F 0PP
020 7287 2881
Wonderful range of fabrics and trimmings at low prices. There are two other branches in the same area.

Camden Passage Antiques Market
Islington Green
London N1

Open Wednesday until 2pm and Saturday until 6pm. Good for old ribbons and trimmings, as well as antique artificial flowers, gifts, dresses and headbands.

Creative Beadcraft
20 Beak Street
London W1F 9RE
020 7629 9964
www.creativebeadcraft.co.uk
Over 3,000 types of beads as well as
feathers, sequins and jewellery.

John Lewis
Oxford Street
London W1A 1EX
020 7629 7711
www.johnlewis.com
Wide range of fabrics and trimmings.

Kleins
5 Noel Street
London W1F 8GD
020 7437 6162
www.kleins.co.uk
Trimmings, clasps, buttons and beads.

Liberty
Regent Street
London W1B 5AH
020 7734 1234
www.liberty.co.uk
Beautiful bridal fabrics and trimmings.

McCulloch & Wallis
25–26 Dering Street
London W1S 1AT
020 7629 0311
www.mcculloch-wallis.co.uk
Silks, lace and trimmings.

V.V. Rouleaux
54 Sloane Square
London SW1W 8AW
020 7730 3125
www.vvrouleaux.com
The ultimate shops for ribbons.

Stationery, paper and card

Most art shops and stationery stores have a good supply of paper and card as well as different materials for decorative details (such as glitter, coloured pens, glues, etc).

Confetti
80–81 Tottenham Court Road
London W1T 4TE
0870 774 7177
www.confetti.com
Everything you need for weddings.

Falkiner Fine Papers
76 Southampton Row
London WC1B 4AR
020 8831 1151

Paperchase
213–215 Tottenham Court Road
London W1T 7PS
020 7467 6200
www.paperchase.co.uk
A fantastic selection of all types of paper, pens and card, including name place cards in a variety of colours. They have numerous branches and a mail order service (call 0161 839 1500).

Smythson
40 New Bond Street
London W1S 2DE
Call 08705 211311 for mail order.
www.smythson.com
Beautifully produced traditional-style wedding stationery.

The Wren Press
Call 020 7351 5887 for mail order.
www.wrenpress.co.uk
Wedding stationery.

Wedding favours

Confetti
A wide selection of traditional and alternative wedding favours. See under Stationery, paper and card for contact details.

Rococo Chocolates
321 Kings Road
London SW3 5EP
020 7352 5857
www.rococochocolates.co.uk
The perfect shop for chocaholics.

Charbonnel et Walker
1 The Royal Arcade
28 Old Bond Street
London W1S 4BT
020 7491 0939
www.charbonnel.co.uk
For delicious favours with a very traditional English look and feel.

Gift ideas

Christofle
10 Hanover Street
London W1R 9HF
020 7491 4004
www.christofle.com

The Dining Room Shop
62–64 White Hart Lane
London SW13 0PZ
020 8878 1020
www.thediningroomshop.co.uk

The Monogrammed Linen Shop
168–170 Walton Street
London SW3 2JL
020 7589 4033
www.monogrammedlinenshop.com

Summerill & Bishop
100 Portland Road
London W11 4LN
020 7221 4566
www.summerillandbishop.com

The Wedding List Company
0870 777 7000
www.theweddinglist.com

Bridal wear
Emma Hope Shoes
53 Sloane Square
London SW1X 8AX
Tel: 020 7259 9566
www.emmahope.co.uk

Joseph Azagury
73 Knightsbridge
London SW1X 7RB
Tel: 020 7259 6887

Virgin Brides
35, King Street
Manchester M2 7AT
0870 0600 436
www.virginbrides.co.uk

General information
**National Weddings Information
Service**
Call 0500 009027 for free information
on wedding services in England,
Scotland and Wales.
www.confetti.co.uk
www.weddingguide.co.uk
Wedding-related websites.

acknowledgements

My biggest thanks go to Polly Wreford for creating such evocative pictures and for her ability to remain so enthusiastic about so many weddings and to discover a fresh approach to each one. Thank you also to her assistant Matt.

A special thank you to Kirsten Robinson, my assistant, for all her help with the deluge of props and for being the perfect bride. Thank you to Ella Ackroyd for giving up a day of her half term to be such a beautiful bridesmaid.

I would like to thank Annabel Morgan, my wonderful editor, for all her support and love of weddings which was so contagious. Also, at Ryland Peters & Small, thank you to Alison Starling, Gabriella Le Grazie, Kate Brunt and Catherine Randy. Thanks to my agent Fiona Lindsay of Limelight Management.

I am very grateful to the many people who kindly lent us their table linens, cutlery, china and glassware. I would like to thank Melanie Sauze for her exquisite sewing, and Jane Cassini and Sandra Lee for all their beautiful keepsakes.

My husband, as always, has been a constant support. Thank you Charles.

The author and publisher would also like to thank everyone who allowed them to photograph in their homes, including Lena Proudlock (Denim in Style, Drews House, Leighterton, Gloucestershire GL8 8UN. Tel/Fax: 01666 890 230), Freddie Daniells and Clare Pike.